Cracking The Female Code

Discover the Hidden Science of Attraction, Gain an Edge in Relationships with Women

Cole Hunter

LM Vintage Publishers

INTRODUCTION

Who understands women?

Well, you are about to. You are holding gold in your hands. The holy grail to understanding women's sexuality and how to use that information to your benefit. There are other books on this subject, but they are either not science-based, sexist, or impractically scientific. Moreover, they do not tie it all together with novel and transformative insights.

This information has been hidden from you by society. Reality and science have been obscured. Women have sexual strategies that we will unveil in this book to benefit you, strategies you likely do not know.

In studying women's attraction, or men's attraction to the opposite sex, and the resulting behaviors, it is essential to remember that evolutionary forces which shape our behaviors and preferences are on a *subconscious* level. Women do not think these things, they behave *without conscious awareness*.

This book is not a novel. It is not written to speak to your emotions. It is concise and focused; it prioritizes delivering clear, informative content rather than engaging solely on an emotional level or extending unnecessarily in length. It is meant to uncover secrets that have been withheld from you. While informal parts, like the beginning and the end, set up and close it out, this book is not written informally purposely.

I will maintain a scholarly tone throughout, offering in-depth insights and thorough coverage of its subject matter. It will educate you on why women are the way they are and how you can attract high-value women (nice, beautiful women) into your life.

This book is compact and a relatively quick read. It delves into necessary technical details, and the language reflects that because it must do so to provide a comprehensive exploration of its subject matter. Because it is entirely based on science, every assertion is backed up by citations from actual scientific studies. The insights you will learn will illuminate women's motivations and enable you to understand how they are, not how society tells you they are, by giving you scientific knowledge and practical suggestions based on science regarding how to use this information to attract high-value women. This book provides a scientifically sound overarching theory of how women's attraction works evolutionarily and how you can use that to your advantage.

This book will explain why women are the way they are in their mating preferences and what a man can do to be more attractive to women. Women are too complicated to understand, right? No, science says they are comprehensible, even if they are more complex in their mating strategies than men. However, to change your approach to women and have more success in having sexual encounters, to have more success in your relationships and your marriage, you need to know the science-based facts, not what society would have you believe about intersexual dynamics.

I have made few observations about the science. Instead, I have presented facts. I have connected the dots regarding the scientific theories to create a cohesive book that explains how we got where we are in society and that evolutionary insights still dictate our relationship to women. It is up to you to decide if you agree with how I connect the dots, but the dots are the anchor points I use throughout the book, which is the science this book is based on.

The intended audience for this book is straight male readers, and thus, it is written from a straight man's perspective to better understand intersexual dynamics and how to navigate them.

But this is not a "red pill" book. It is based on facts. It is not misogynistic or homophobic. There is no excuse to hate women or think them inferior, ever. It is not moral to judge LGBTQAI+ people, although they are not the intended audience of this book. You can and should use this information ethically.

This book is written for men to better understand the factual realities of intersexual dynamics, and how they have come to benefit women more and more, though there are many areas where men still have the advantage. The objective is to learn how those dynamics influence men's relationships with women. We will also delve into some of what a man can do to understand and navigate the complexities of intersexual relationships to their benefit.

The Science

This book and its conclusions rely mostly on evolutionary psychology.

Evolutionary psychology is a scientific approach that seeks to understand human behavior and cognition through the lens of evolutionary theory. It explores how psychological traits and behaviors have evolved as adaptations to solve problems related to survival and reproduction.

The central idea is that many aspects of human psychology and behavior, such as mate selection, can be better understood by considering its evolutionary origins and the selective pressures that shaped them.

Evolutionary psychologists study how natural selection has influenced the development of cognitive processes and behavioral tendencies that contribute to human survival and reproductive success.

This book studies evolutionary mating psychology, which is the study of sex and sexual behavior within evolutionary psychology. It can also be referred to more descriptively as the evolutionary psychology of human mating. This field investigates how sexual behaviors, preferences, and strategies have evolved to adapt and promote reproductive success.

Evolutionary mating psychology explains why men and women relate the way they do to each other intersexually and in the "dating marketplace."

The dating marketplace can be understood scientifically as the social and psychological landscape where individuals seek, attract, and form relationships with romantic partners. This concept draws from evolutionary psychology and sociology to analyze how individuals make decisions about mate selection based on various factors such as physical attractiveness, personality traits, social status, resources, and reproductive fitness.

From an evolutionary perspective, the dating marketplace reflects the competition and strategies involved in mate selection, which is shaped by natural and sexual selection pressures. It involves assessing potential partners based on perceived benefits and costs in terms of reproductive success and the long-term viability of the relationship.

In a broader societal context, the dating marketplace also encompasses cultural norms, technological advancements like dating apps, and demographic trends that influence how people meet and form relationships. Studying the dating marketplace scientifically involves examining these complex dynamics to understand the factors influencing romantic interactions and partner choices.

What Women Say They Want

What women say they want and what they do want do not match up in our modern, social construct. From an evolutionary standpoint, the sexes are meant to complement each other, not be the same. Despite societal shifts towards gender equality and changing gender roles, evolutionary predispositions still influence mate preferences and attraction dynamics.

Studies in evolutionary psychology, such as those conducted by David Buss and Martie Haselton, have explored mate preferences across cultures and found consistent patterns indicating women's attraction to traits associated with resource acquisition, social dominance, and physical prowess. These traits, often labeled as traditionally masculine, have been linked to indicators of genetic fitness and reproductive success throughout human history.

This has made it harder for men because women's increasing economic independence and social empowerment have reshaped traditional gender dynamics, granting them the freedom to demand qualities in partners that encompass both provisioning and physical attractiveness. Research by Fugère et al. (2015) highlights a shift in mate preferences among women, emphasizing traits related to both resource provisioning and physical attractiveness. This trend reflects a desire for partners who can provide material support and security while possessing qualities associated with genetic fitness and attractiveness. Today, a man has to have both to some degree, so not to be easily discarded, where provisioning used to be enough.

Birth control alters this natural state of attraction to provisioning to a large degree. The proliferation of birth control has fundamentally altered the dynamics of intimate relationships, creating a landscape where men must adapt to survive. While the changes may be daunting, they also present opportunities for men to get what they want (relationships, sex) by using researched knowledge of women and how they operate from an evidence-based place, alongside improving themselves to meet what women have evolved to want over eons.

In the chapters that follow, we will explore in detail the specific ways in which the widespread use of birth control has reshaped the sexual marketplace, examining the impact on men's experiences, perceptions of masculinity, and strategies for navigating this new terrain. Through careful analysis, we will uncover the enduring consequences of birth control on male-female dynamics and consider the implications for the future of gender relations and what you can do about it for your benefit.

Before we go on, we should define what men are attracted to universally from an evolutionary psychology perspective, though this book is about what women are attracted to in men, this is still important to define. You may be attracted to any number of attributes in a woman, but men's attraction to certain traits in women are primary. If you can attract a high value woman with these traits you will do so almost invariably, to the extent that you can. These attributes are reproductive fitness indicators.

Research suggests that men are most often drawn to physical features such as youthfulness, clear skin, and an hourglass figure, as these characteristics are linked to fertility and health (Buss, 1999; Singh, 1993). Additionally, cues of reproductive value such as facial symmetry, not being overweight, with a good waist-to-hip (WHR) ratio are important. WHR means that the circumference of the waist is about 70-80% of the circumference of the hips. All of these play a significant role in attractiveness judgments (Thornhill & Gangestad, 1999; Singh, 1993; Dixson et al., 2003)

Evolutionarily, these preferences are believed to enhance the likelihood of successful reproduction and the passing on of advantageous genes to offspring, and so these preferences are perpetuated across generations. Also, behaviors such as kindness, nurturance, and warmth in women are valued traits, potentially indicating good parenting abilities and support in raising offspring (Buss, 1999). Evolutionary psychology suggests that many aspects of what men find attractive are deeply rooted in biological imperatives shaped by millennia of human evolution.

CHAPTER 1

It's All about Reproduction

Have you ever wondered what your purpose is? Did you think it was to make the world a better place? Feed the hungry? Become wealthy? Write a book? It could be all or none of these things.

However, science points to survival and reproduction. The reason to survive is to reproduce, so the main point of existence is to reproduce.

Maybe you would say your main driving purpose is to have a child?

Ding! Right answer!

Full disclosure, I am a Christian. I believe the purpose of life is to know and love Jesus. But this is not a Christian book whatsoever. I am a Christian who knows evolution is a fact, science is real, and it dictates the reality of the physical world. We do not live inside the Bible.

All of your goals are reasonable, some of them even noble, perhaps. But all those goals are related to your ultimate purpose biologically. Your ultimate purpose, scientifically, is to reproduce.

It is the base upon which everything is built. As a man, you go to college to get a degree and get a good job. You make some money, you do it for yourself, but you subconsciously are doing it to find a mate. To be worthy of one.

Some of you do not want children. That is fine. But it does not change the fact that nature's reason for existence is for you to successfully reproduce.

A man and a woman meet in college at a party. They go back to his apartment, and they start making out.

The young woman is named Denise, and the young man is named David.

David kisses Denise passionately and undoes her blouse. He cradles her breasts into his hand and lifts her skirt. She breaths more heavily. He slides her panties off and unzips his jeans pulling out his member.

She kisses him hard, and they have sex.

Do either of those college kids want a baby? Do they consciously want to reproduce? No. They have futures they dream to achieve, and they don't know each other all that well. The last thing they are thinking of is a baby. Yet they find themselves naked, him on top of her, and sharing bodily fluids. Why? Because it feels good. Why does it feel good? It feels good because the body wants to reproduce whether we consciously want to or not, and our behaviors follow that desire.

Denise probably used some form of birth control. Women who do not want to get pregnant use contraception 88% of the time (Guttmacher Institute). However, all that proves is that they consciously do not want a child. Their body speaks a different language and demands that they act upon their urges. It speaks the language of reproduction.

However, the contraception Denise used was probably not a condom.

According to a large CDC study, during 2011–2015, only 23.8% of American women and only 33.7% of American men aged 15–44 in the study used a condom at last sexual intercourse in the past 12 months (CDC).

In the study, 25.8% said the condom was used for only part of the time during intercourse. This means you can subtract approximately a quarter off the above low condom use rate because they started but did not finish using a condom.

Admittedly, this study includes some longer dating couples, but it still shows that condoms are not likely to be used the majority of the time. And yes, some have the wherewithal to use a condom.

But why do most not use a condom? They likely utilize another contraceptive method like hormonal birth control because a condom must be used when the mind is off and the passions are on. Because when the conscious mind is not in-volved, the instinct is to reproduce. The sex feels better without a condom.

Pleasure is nature's reward system for getting us to copulate even when no child is desired.

So, sex is pleasurable because it is meant to induce reproduction, even if subconsciously. Your evolved psychology and body want to have children, even if your mind does not.

Most of what you do revolves around women. You are either married and trying to stay that way, trying to find a way to cheat, or looking for a divorce to find another mate.

You may be single, and you are looking for sex. You may not be looking for sex, but you are looking at pornography to satisfy your desire to procreate through self-satisfaction. Perhaps you are not doing any of these things. Even so, you will be doing them soon enough, after your "break" from these activities.

Why do you try to get a good job? Why do you try to dress nicely outside of work? Why do you drive fast and take risks?

You do these or other things that drive you. You do them to attract or keep a mate. Even if they seem you do them for yourself.

According to a study published in the *Journal of Personality and Social Psychology,* men often engage in behaviors aimed at attracting potential romantic partners, including displays of social status, physical attractiveness, and resources (Buss, 1989). These behaviors can be influenced by subconscious factors such as evolutionary instincts and societal norms.

Remember, reproduction is the reason you exist.

CHAPTER 2

What Women Want

Steve met Stacy at a bar on Fifth Street in Austin, Texas. It was a dive bar, the kind of place that hung old bottle caps in the shape of Texas in front of the restrooms and had a bar made out of wood with varnish long scuffed off.

Stacy was twenty-five, thin, a brunette with freckles and a curvy waist. She worked in marketing. She had left work, and this bar was the closest to her apartment. She always got attention at bars but, after a stressful day at work, she did not want any guys hitting on her so she went there knowing it would be sparsely populated.

Steve was at the bar when he saw Stacy take a seat two bar stools down. She was the only one there. Steve, an attorney dressed in a dark suit, had gotten out of a tough court case earlier.

He did not live close. Like Stacy, he was divorced and occasionally lonely at 35. He thought he might have less competition getting a girl to bed for the night if he came somewhere with less competition. It seemed to him that he would hit the jackpot.

He saw Stacy. Her blue eyes shone across the dimly lit bar as she glanced absently at him and then back down at her drink. He decided then that he would try to sleep with her, but Stacy was just looking to have a drink and leave.

Steve said, "What are you doing in a dive like this?"

She was annoyed and looked up at him, "I could ask the same about you."

"Well, I had a hard day in court, and we had a bad day in the case, so I decided to have a drink and..."

Steve decided to be bold, knowing he could be shot down.

"...to see about trying out my new argument on whoever walked through that door, and that happened to be you. Would you mind me trying it out with you?"

Stacy now looked interested in talking, and Steve could tell.

"Go on," she said.

"This man stole a car, my client, and I thought I would bring a witness up who would corroborate that he was not stealing a car at that time."

"Sounds like a good idea," Stacy said.

"Right, his alibi was he was not stealing the car he is accused of stealing because he was out stealing another car."

Stacy smiled and said, "How would that help?"

"Well it would prove that he wasn't stealing the vehicle, but it would create doubt in the veracity of his alibi."

Stacy looked down and then up at Steve. Her hips swiveled to face him warily, and she played with her hair. She smiled.

"So, a bad argument then?"

She laughed. "Yeah, it's pretty bad."

"What's your name?"

"Stacy."

"Stacy, now that you're a part of this case, if I had you on the witness stand, and you're under oath, remember, and I asked you if you would go have a late dinner with me, would you be honest?"

Stacy nodded her head.

"Okay, and since you're still under oath, do you like sushi?"

Stacy laughed hard at this. "Yes, what's your name?"

"Steve. Let's get out of here. There's a sushi place across the street."

"Okay, let's go."

They left and ate sushi and had a bit of saki. They were not drunk but quite tipsy. They laughed, and Stacy no longer felt stressed. She thought Steve was very handsome and was drawn to him.

Steve helped her from the booth and offered to walk her home the three blocks. On her doorstep, he stopped close and kissed her. She kissed back.

Steve had a desire to bend her over the rails on those stairs. But he did not, of course. He casually said, "I guess that's it then.

I enjoyed meeting you, Stacy. I haven't had as much fun with a woman as I did with you in a year. Off the record."

She giggled and said, "Would you come up for another drink for a few minutes, Steve?"

Steve did, and he was able to bend her quite deftly over her bed, and, to his great satisfaction, her body looked better naked than clothed. The next morning, as she slept, he snuck out and never spoke to Stacy again.

This fictional vignette helps illustrate what women want and how men use that to get what they want.

Stacy was not interested in Steve, but his confidence made her pay attention to him. Women value confidence in men. According to a study published in the *Journal of Personality and Social Psychology*, women are often attracted to men who display confidence in social situations (Buss, 1989).

Steve tried to speak with Stacy even though she was not initially open to it. According to a study published in the journal *Evolution and Human Behavior*, women are often attracted to men with a good sense of humor (Li et al., 2009). Steve brought her into a humorous conversation by introducing her to the client who stole the car and then used that as a pretext to get her to spend more time with him at the sushi bar.

However, if Steve were a janitor, this would not have worked. Stacy was also attracted to Steve and receptive to his humor because of his status as a lawyer. Research published in the *Journal of Personality and Social Psychology* indicates that women are often attracted to men with high social status (Townsend & Levy, 1990).

Stacy initially thought Steve was average-looking, but because of his humor, status, and confidence, she found him too hard to resist.

CHAPTER 3

Who Has the Advantage?

Later, we will discuss strategies for becoming more confident, having more status, being funnier, bolder, assertive, and ultimately more attractive to women.

Alternatively, you can learn how to fake these attributes. Why? These are the things women value: the pretty ones who are nice and the high-value ones you want.

Confidence is a behavior that can be learned, and so are most of the behaviors that women find attractive. You can pretend while you work on improving yourself, in turn making yourself into a high-value man.

One example of a learned behavior is to create rapport with a woman with confidence and then use humor to attract her further.

According to a study published in the journal *Evolution and Human Behavior*, women tend to perceive men they find attractive as funnier, even if others do not find their jokes particularly humorous (Bressler & Balshine, 2006). This creates a positive feedback loop, so if you can be confident, you can turn your interactions with a woman into humor. Status must be earned, but it can be exaggerated, as can most of these behaviors. To do so is no worse than a woman putting on makeup to cover her blemishes.

You may be asking where looks come in. Well, they come in second for a woman and first for a man. Research published in the journal *Evolutionary Psychology* indicates that men tend to value youth and physical attractiveness in women as important factors in mate selection (Buss, 1989) . Additionally, studies have shown that men may prioritize youth in women because it is associated with reproductive potential and the ability to bear healthy offspring (Singh, 1993). Furthermore, attractiveness in women is often defined by features such as waist-to-hip ratio and symmetry, as these traits are perceived as indicators of genetic health and fertility (Singh, 1993; Swami et al., 2006). According to research published in the journal *Evolution and Human Behavior*, men tend to prioritize physical attractiveness as the primary factor in mate selection. At the same time, women may consider it as a secondary or less significant factor (Buss, 1989).

Men value youth and beauty in a woman. They want a woman who can reliably and safely reproduce, which enables an evaluation of genetic health for offspring.

Women do value looks, even if far less than men. This is especially true during ovulation. However, as I have said, they do not value it to the degree that men do.

Women do not value youth per se because even if men produce sperm that is less viable as they age, they can reproduce throughout their lifetime, and so youth in a man is not essential at all for reproduction. It takes time for men to accrue the resources and status that women are attracted to. In fact, women prefer somewhat older men. According to a study published in the journal *Evolutionary Psychology*, women tend to prefer partners who are approximately three to five years older than themselves (Kenrick & Keefe, 1992).

This is not to say that most 20-year-old women want to date 50-year-old men. But this is why a typical 50-year-old man is more attractive than an average 50-year-old woman. The opposite sex defines what is attractive to the other sex.

So, men in their twenties and sixties find women in their twenties attractive. This is due to evolution and biology. Being attracted to a twenty-five-year-old woman at seventy does not make you a dirty old man. It makes you a man. One does not have to act a dirty old man; but a man cannot help the attraction. He may not admit it to anyone, but he is hardwired to find a young, pretty girl attractive, no matter his age. Nor does it make sense to label women as gold diggers for being attracted to resources. By their very nature, they are attracted to men with status and resources. A woman may consider a man possessing "resources" as simply making more money than she does or contributing a healthy share to their combined finances.

Women are drawn to men who provide because our hunter-gatherer ancestors who were successful in reproducing were good hunters or providers of resources. Men hunted, and women gathered. Research shows that, in many hunter-gatherer societies, men traditionally engaged in hunting activities, while women played a significant role in gathering plant foods and other resources (Kelly, 1995).

Women depended on men to bring home the "meat." This is true with money, despite what feminism would have you believe women prioritize. Not all feminism is bad. Some of it is good, but much of it denies science and says that much of everything is socially determined when evolutionary adaptations have largely determined behavior.

I will give my only caveat to that here. This book is about women and men in the aggregate and their aggregate behaviors. There is still room for individual responses to differ based on unique circumstances. However, those are the exceptions, not the rule. Yes, there is a societal influence that can bend, but not break, these hardwired behaviors and impossible-to-deny influences. For instance, it was once thought that women could not be CEOs and could only cook, clean, and take care of their children. This is incorrect because women can make great CEOs. This is the case even though women in our evolutionary past almost exclusively gathered during hunter-gatherer days, while men hunted and brought home "the meat." Now, women can bring home "the meat" (money).

But women who earn more divorce men. Women who earn significantly more than their husbands are about 50% more likely to divorce them. Conversely, men who earn significantly more than their wives do not face a higher likelihood of divorce, as noted in research by Killewald and Gough (2010). Women still have the hardwired desire for a mate who makes more money. We can change how we play the game, but the evolutionary rules for attraction remain the same, which is the basis of this book.

Mate Value

In evolutionary psychology, mate value pertains to an individual's composite desirability as a potential partner, and for men this includes various attributes such as physical attractiveness, social status, resources, intelligence, and personality traits (Buss, 1989). It reflects an individual's reproductive fitness and the perceived likelihood of successful reproduction and offspring survival (Buss & Schmitt, 1993). Mate value theory posits that these traits have evolved due to their adaptive significance in mating strategies and reproductive success (Buss, 2003). Individuals with higher mate value are typically more sought after as mates. They offer potential partners greater reproductive benefits and genetic quality (Buss, 2006).

Women have the power in mating when they are young. Nothing is more powerful in mating than a young, pretty woman. But men ordinarily have a severe advantage as women and men age. Men have traditionally had their pick on who to partner with if they are of reasonably high mate value.

Men can overcome lower mate values by working hard to earn more money, working out, and dressing well, among other things. Women can use Botox and other cosmetic devices to appear younger, but these are less reliable and durable than methods men possess to remain attractive as they age.

But this doesn't tell the whole story because hormonal birth control and the advent and popularity of online dating have tilted power back toward women, as we will delve into. I posit that women have equal advantage when looking for a mate until their early forties, and not just when they are young, due to artificial constructs. These constructs show that society and even medication can influence the level that evolutionary adaptations influence behavior. But this is an example of bending evolutionary dictates, it does not break them, nothing can. We will delve into how they only bend them, not break them and how you can use that to your advantage. They very much still dictate behavior.

Men have equal advantage after women's mid-twenties peak, when they hit their thirties, when before which women have the advantage. The sexes are equal until early middle age, after that men have a slight advantage. But after menopause men have the total advantage.

This is not true for high mate value men. Evolution has overcome these society influenced changes for them. It is just the average man's traditionally natural advantage after women's peak has eroded somewhat as it has been hampered by these artificial, societal, or medical interventions in favor of women. This is not to say that women do not deserve to use birth control to control their reproduction, it is to say that men need to be aware of how it has altered some of the natural advantage they possess at a given age. Although online dating has been a disaster for both sexes, especially men, which we will delve into later.

This all may seem unfair to men, as women have the advantage already when they are younger in mate choice and just by being a female. But that is not totally true because women used to be subjugated by men. They deserve their reproductive prerogative. However, what is unfair is that as they have been given, rightfully so, their own agency and autonomy, men have far less than their natural advantage in the mating marketplace now. It is tilted in favor of women through the majority of both sexes reproductive years on average.

Life's not fair, it never has been. But if you are a high-value man, that is you have high mate value, then you can retain the advantage that nature has gifted you in your thirties, forties, and beyond.

Let us delve into how birth control determines a woman's mate choices.

CHAPTER 4
(Birth) Control

Birth control revolutionized the dynamics between men and women. Introduced in 1960, it swiftly gained popularity, becoming the predominant method of contraception by 1965 (Smith, 2010). This advent coincided with the sexual revolution of the mid-1960s, marked by a liberalization of attitudes towards pre-marital sex and sexual norms (Jones, 2015). Women were no longer constrained by the societal expectation to abstain from sex until marriage to avoid pregnancy. The availability of birth control relieved them of the fear of unintended pregnancies, leading to increased sexual activity (Smith, 2010). Consequently, women were empowered to make choices about their sexual lives without the looming threat of unwanted pregnancies.

This also meant that women did not need to marry during their peak mate value years, if at all, due to fear of pregnancy with no partner, and this artificially extended their mate value for years as men had to accept this shift in order to mate and marry.

As the availability of birth control has facilitated greater sexual freedom, it has increased the prevalence of multiple sexual partners. Studies indicate that both men and women who have a higher number of sexual partners are more likely to engage in infidelity within committed relationships (Brewster & Tillman, 2012; Mark, Janssen, & Milhausen, 2011). Research suggests that women who have a higher number of sexual partners, such as more than five, are significantly more likely to engage in infidelity within committed relationships, with some studies suggesting this likelihood can be up to three times higher than those with fewer partners (Brewster & Tillman, 2012; Mark, Janssen, & Milhausen, 2011). It is likely that the liberalization of sexual attitudes accompanying the availability of birth control has contributed to this increase in infidelity among individuals with multiple sexual partners (Mark et al., 2011). None of this is meant to infer that women or men do not have a right to multiple partners, however, this is still good data just to know.

Women's Evolved Preference for Men with Resources

Women throughout humanity's existence have been attracted to men primarily due to resources. Birth control did not stop that attraction as being central to mating choices, but it did make women less necessitous of provisioning from men, thus making women less attracted to men for provisioning. Nevertheless, recent studies continue to support the notion that women prioritize a man's resources and provisioning in long-term mating. For example, research by Conroy-Beam et al. (2015) found that women's mate preferences for long-term partners are influenced by cues of economic resources, such as income and occupational status.

Additionally, Feinberg et al. (2012) demonstrated that women's preference for resource investment in a partner is heightened during the fertile phase of the menstrual cycle, suggesting an adaptive function of these preferences in reproductive decision-making. Moreover, studies utilizing online dating platforms have shown that women tend to prioritize socioeconomic status and education level when selecting partners for long-term relationships (Hitsch et al., 2010). These findings underscore the enduring relevance of resource-related traits in women's mate preferences for long-term mating strategies in contemporary society.

Provisioning by Men Lessens in Importance

Thirty-two percent of women worked outside the home in 1950, but by 1970, this figure had risen to 43%. By 2010, 58% of women worked outside the home (U.S. Bureau of Labor Statistics).

The implications of women's increased economic autonomy are profound and have placed men at a disadvantage in the sexual marketplace. This is not to say a woman should not have a right to work, we are talking about mating advantage. As women have become more financially self-sufficient, their reliance on men for resources has decreased. This shift has disrupted the traditional evolutionary draw men held over women in economic provisioning, leaving many men sidelined and undervalued in relationships.

For men, the erosion of their role as primary providers has undermined their status and bargaining power in the mating game. Women still desire partners who can provide, yet they no longer need to depend on men for financial stability. This gives women a significant advantage, as they can afford to be more selective in choosing their partners, while men face heightened competition for the attention and affection of potential mates. It is harder to impress a woman with an average paycheck when she can readily get her own. According to a study conducted by the *American Sociological Association*, women initiate approximately 75% of divorces in the United States. It is harder to keep a woman when she has such vast economic options.

The rise of female empowerment has challenged conventional notions of masculinity, leaving many men struggling to define their roles and identities in a society where their traditional roles are no longer as valued or necessary. This is the case even as women still desire men with conventionally masculine traits, such as provisioning. But by lessening the need for evolutionarily adapted dependence on male provisioning, women find it easier to discard men. Men have a higher sex drive and need for regular sex, which makes them less likely to discard women and puts them at a disadvantage.

But evolutionary psychology, which has developed over a hundred thousand years cannot be undone in a few decades. Women still find a man who offers provisioning attractive.

CHAPTER 5

Unraveling the Intricacies of Female Mate Choice

To better understand birth control, it helps to better understand what women may experience when naturally cycling. To comprehend the intricacies of female mate choice and sexual behavior, it is important to look at evolutionary psychology.

The ovulatory shift hypothesis is captivating, shedding light on the fluctuations in female mate preferences across the menstrual cycle. This hypothesis, rooted in the idea that women's preferences for certain mate traits may vary cyclically, offers valuable insights into women's adaptive strategies to enhance their reproductive success.

At the core of the ovulatory shift hypothesis lies the premise that women's mate preferences are influenced by hormonal fluctuations, particularly during ovulation (Gangestad, Thornhill, & Garver-Apgar, 2005). Research suggests that during the fertile phase of the menstrual cycle, women demonstrate a heightened preference for traits associated with genetic fitness and good genes. This preference shift is believed to be driven by an evolutionary urge to secure optimal mates during peak fertility, thereby increasing the likelihood of successful reproduction and the transmission of advantageous traits to offspring.

Traits such as masculinity, physical attractiveness, and dominance are prioritized during ovulation, reflecting women's unconscious quest for partners possessing indicators of genetic quality and reproductive fitness.

Research in evolutionary psychology supports the concept of women's dual mating strategy. According to studies such as Gangestad and Thornhill's research (1997), women tend to show preferences for traits associated with good genetic quality during periods of peak fertility. In contrast, studies by Buss (1989) and Kenrick et al. (1990) suggest that women prioritize traits like kindness and reliability in long-term partners, reflecting a strategy focused on securing paternal investment for offspring welfare during non-fertile phases. This dual strategy is seen as adaptive, allowing women to maximize reproductive success through both genetic quality and parental investment.

Empirical support for the ovulatory shift hypothesis stems from numerous studies demonstrating predictable variations in women's mate preferences across the menstrual cycle. For instance, research has revealed that women exhibit a greater preference for masculine facial features, symmetrical body shapes, and dominant behaviors during the fertile phase compared to non-fertile phases (Haselton & Gangestad, 2006). Experimental paradigms, including mate choice tasks and hypothetical mate selection scenarios, consistently indicate that women prefer cues associated with genetic fitness and good genes during ovulation.

These findings suggest that women may strategically allocate reproductive resources toward partners offering the greatest reproductive benefits during periods of high fertility.

The ovulatory shift hypothesis holds profound implications for our understanding of human mating behavior, shedding light on women's adaptive strategies to navigate the complex landscape of mate choice.

Women may maximize their chances of securing high-quality mates and producing offspring with advantageous traits by exhibiting a heightened preference for cues associated with genetic fitness and reproductive potential during ovulation. Moreover, the hypothesis offers insights into the mechanisms underlying specific aspects of female sexual behavior, such as extra-pair mating (cheating) and mate-switching during ovulation (Miller & Maner, 2012). Understanding the impact of hormonal fluctuations on mate preferences deepens our understanding of human mating dynamics, highlighting the interplay between biology, psychology, and culture.

Women Don't Need Men (As Much as They Used To)

Clearly, women's reliance on men has shifted significantly over time. With evolving societal norms and gender roles undergoing radical transformations—particularly since the introduction of hormonal birth control—men now face the implications of a world where their traditional roles as providers and protectors are becoming much less important.

One of the fundamental distinctions between men and women lies in their respective sex drives, which can be proven by research, despite what you are told by the women's empowerment community that says women and men are the same. There are exceptions, but research consistently indicates that men generally have a higher libido than women, partly influenced by biological factors such as testosterone levels (Baumeister et al., 2001). This inherent difference in sexual desire has historically positioned men as the pursuers, driven by their primal instincts to fulfill reproductive potential and satisfy innate urges. Men know this to be true already from personal experience.

Evolutionary psychology sheds light on why women often assume the role of the choosier sex in mate selection. Biologically, women invest more in reproduction, both in terms of resources required for pregnancy and the risks associated with childbirth. Consequently, women tend to be more discerning in choosing partners, prioritizing traits that signal genetic fitness, resourcefulness, and commitment (Buss, 1989).

This inherent selectivity poses a challenge for men in the sexual arena, requiring them to compete for the attention and approval of women who wield significant choice power. In a world where women have greater autonomy to pursue their desires and goals, you must strive harder to demonstrate your worthiness to potential partners.

Another sobering reality for men is the attractiveness gap between the sexes. Before birth control, women looked less at physical appearance than they do now. Research consistently demonstrates that a more significant proportion of women are perceived as attractive than men (Feingold, 1990). In simple terms, while more women find the average man unattractive, men still find the average woman attractive. This disparity further skews the balance of power in favor of women, who are inundated with attention and admiration from men vying for their affection.

For men, this translates to fiercer competition and a narrower pool of potential partners, as women gravitate towards individuals exhibiting the most desirable traits. To surmount this challenge, you must focus on cultivating qualities that set you apart, whether intelligence, humor, ambition, or emotional intelligence.

You must adapt your dating and relationship strategies to thrive in the modern sexual marketplace.

CHAPTER 6
Birth Control and Marriage

Birth control significantly changes a woman's attraction to her partner. If you are married, thinking about getting married, or considering a long-term partner, you do not want to waste your life with someone who is with you because her hormones have been altered, and she would not be with you when off birth control.

For women who met their eventual husbands while on birth control, there are notable shifts in partner preferences and attraction dynamics.

Women on birth control pills exhibit mate preferences similar to those observed during pregnancy, as hormonal contraceptives mimic physiological cues associated with pregnancy (Roberts et al., 2004). This can lead women to prioritize qualities in men that suggest stability and reliability, akin to the preferences for supportive traits seen during pregnancy, influencing their mate choices. Women not using hormonal contraceptives typically show more preferences for men displaying indicators of genetic fitness, such as masculinity and physical attractiveness (Penton-Voak et al., 1999; Gangestad & Simpson, 2000).

When women meet their husbands while on birth control, it sets a unique backdrop for examining how contraceptive use shapes long-term partner preferences. Research suggests that hormonal contraceptives can influence women's attraction patterns, altering their perception of potential mates (Roberts et al., 2018). This alteration stems from the hormonal changes induced by birth control, which can impact women's preferences for certain traits in a partner.

Studies have shown that women who meet their partners while on birth control may experience shifts in attraction preferences over time, particularly after discontinuing contraceptive use (Alvergne et al., 2009). The hormones present in birth control pills can influence women's perceptions of male facial attractiveness, leading them to prioritize different traits than they might otherwise. As a result, once women cease using birth control, their preferences may realign with their natural hormonal fluctuations, potentially affecting their perception of their husband's attractiveness. This has implications for you if you are married. If you are not married, be vigilant that your wife-to-be is attracted to you for more than your provisioning capacity. Remember, resources are not as central to attraction for women as they used to be. Do you want your wife to be attracted to you viscerally, or only for provisioning with resources, or future resource potential?

Research indicates that women often prioritize resource potential when selecting long-term partners, which can lead them to marry men who offer stability and economic security (Buss, 1989; Buss & Schmitt, 1993). These partners may differ from the more masculine men they may have dated before, who might have been perceived as more sexually attractive and assertive but less reliable in terms of long-term commitment (Gangestad & Simpson, 2000). However, over time, some women may become dissatisfied with their choice as they perceive their partners as lacking in masculine qualities or other attributes that were not initially apparent (Buss & Schmitt, 1993).

Thus understanding the influence of birth control on partner attraction is crucial for comprehending relationship dynamics, especially for couples who met during contraceptive use. Research suggests that changes in attraction preferences can impact relationship satisfaction and longevity (Little et al., 2008). Couples may find themselves navigating shifts in perceived attractiveness, which could potentially influence intimacy and overall relationship quality.

What Are the Implications of This for You?

Research indicates a notable trend: women who discontinue birth control after meeting their spouse are more likely to initiate divorces. Studies such as those conducted by Klapilová et al. (2014) suggest a significant correlation between changes in hormonal contraception and relationship dynamics, highlighting the complex interplay between biology and relationship outcomes.

The intersection of birth control use and partner attraction is a multifaceted phenomenon with implications for romantic relationships. This is why it is essential to meet a woman not on hormonal birth control or to ask her to use an alternate method before you marry to test the strength of the relationship. If you are already married, maybe you should encourage your wife to try the copper IUD, or use condoms, get a vasectomy, or your wife could get tubal litigation. Any non-hormonal birth control methods will give you a chance to evaluate whether the relationship is viable and authentic because hormones largely determine sexual attraction.

One example of where hormones influence people is their sexual orientation. They are the main reason someone turns out to be gay. Hormones are widely recognized to play a significant role in sexual orientation. Research indicates that prenatal exposure to androgens, such as testosterone, during critical periods of fetal development can impact the development of brain structures related to sexual orientation (Hines, 2011). This suggests a biological basis for variations in sexual orientation influenced by hormonal factors.

And hormonal birth control changes women's hormones related to their sexuality. Hormonal birth control methods, such as oral contraceptives and hormonal IUDs, impact sexual hormones by introducing synthetic forms of estrogen and/or progestin. These synthetic hormones mimic natural hormones involved in the menstrual cycle and reproductive processes.

Estrogen and progestin influence sexual hormones by regulating the menstrual cycle, affecting libido, and influencing mood and sexual behavior (Bitzer et al., 2016; Wiegratz & Kuhl, 2006). For example, estrogen levels can enhance sexual desire, while progestin may have a dampening effect due to its role in preparing the uterus for potential pregnancy (Davis et al., 2005).

These hormonal contraceptives can alter natural hormone levels, potentially affecting sexual function and satisfaction (Wiegratz & Kuhl, 2006). Research indicates that hormonal contraceptives can impact sexual desire and arousal patterns due to their influence on hormone levels critical to sexual health (Bitzer et al., 2016).

Hormonal birth control methods exert their effects on sexual hormones by introducing synthetic estrogen and progestin, thereby regulating menstrual cycles and influencing sexual desire and function.

If hormones can be a causative factor in making someone homosexual, they certainly can influence your wife's desire to be with you.

Hormonal fluctuations throughout life, including during puberty and adulthood, can influence sexual desire, attraction patterns, and behaviors (Breedlove, 2010).

You want to see if your wife, as she is with natural hormones, wants to be with you.

They lay in bed one night and John placed his hand on Shelly's thigh, creeping up toward her panties.

She pushed his hand away. He could feel the disgust at his touch through her fingertips.

"Shelly, what is the matter?"

"I don't know John, I – I just am not in the mood to have sex."

"You aren't in the mood to have sex, then how are we going to have a baby?"

"John, I just don't, I think I'm not in love with you anymore."

John took a deep breath. He was confused.

"Why – what did I do, is it another man?"

"No, I just can't feel anything for you – I'm just not attracted to you anymore. Everything you do annoys me, even how you're acting now. It feels pathetic."

She softened, reaching for his hand. John pulled his hand away.

"I'm not saying we should get a divorce, maybe we should go to counseling."

John said, "I read an article that said that stopping birth control can change the way you feel about your husband."

"Oh, John, how could a pill do that."

They stayed together, under tense circumstances. What John and Shelly did not know was that she was already pregnant. A month after Shelly got pregnant, they were on a date.

"I love you, John. You are everything I could want for our baby girl and for me."

"Shelly, a month ago, you didn't know if you loved me. I've been looking at divorce lawyers. I went on this date to tell you I was leaving you, but now you tell me you love me again?"

Shelly started crying. "I don't know why I acted that way. It must have been because we didn't get pregnant immediately. I am so sorry, John."

"Shelly, I love you too. Was it another man?"

"No, of course not."

"Were you attracted to another man?"

Shelly thought, and then she said, "Yes, Tyler at work. But I never did anything about it."

"But you don't feel that way about him now?"

"Of course not, I only love you. You've changed, you are more the man you were when we first married."

John was confused as he was the same man he was a month ago.

"Shelly, I think it could have been getting off of the birth control."

"That's ridiculous, John. We know who we love, a medicine doesn't influence that."

John did not know for sure what it was, and when Shelly kissed him, he did not care. She touched him, and they made passionate love, more passionate than when trying to get pregnant, right there, inside the car like teenagers.

CHaPTer 7

Women Don't Want Average Men (Maybe You're Just Average)

A noticeable shift has occurred in women's dependency on men. This transformation has been particularly pronounced since the widespread adoption of hormonal birth control, leading to substantial changes in societal norms and gender roles. As a result, men find themselves confronting a reality where their traditional roles as providers and protectors are progressively diminishing. There are many areas that give women advantages, where women do not need men as much as men need women.

Consequently, men face heightened competition and a narrower pool of potential partners. To navigate this challenge successfully, you must focus on cultivating attributes to become a high-value man and distinguish yourself from the crowd of average men, whether through intellect, humor, ambition, emotional intelligence, or other attributes we will discuss.

The Rise of Selectivity: How Birth Control Shapes Women's Preferences for High-Value Men

Throughout human history, women have faced the evolutionary imperative to select mates with the greatest likelihood of reproductive success. This has traditionally translated into a preference for partners who demonstrate traits associated with genetic fitness, resourcefulness, and commitment. However, the advent of birth control has fundamentally altered the landscape of mate choice, allowing women to be more discerning in their selection process.

Freed from the constraints of unplanned pregnancy, women are empowered to pursue relationships on their terms, with a newfound emphasis on qualities associated with high-value mates. Women are no longer compelled to settle for mates who merely fulfill basic criteria for reproductive viability. Instead, they are free to prioritize qualities such as ambition, intelligence, emotional intelligence, physical attractiveness, and compatibility in their search for high-value partners who offer the greatest potential for long-term fulfillment and happiness.

Birth control has fueled a rise in selectivity among women, reshaping their preferences and expectations in the search for high-value partners.

The Pursuit of High-Value Traits

Research suggests that women's preferences for romantic partners may be influenced by various factors, including social, cultural, and evolutionary considerations. In a post-birth control world, women may be more inclined to seek partners with traits associated with high social status, success, and desirability. (Fisman et al., 2006)

This may manifest in a preference for partners who exhibit confidence, ambition, physical attractiveness, and assertiveness, as well as those who demonstrate kindness, empathy, and emotional stability. Evolutionary psychology has shown that women are attracted to traits associated with physical and psychological strength, as well as the ability to provide and protect. (Buss, 1989)

The rise of selectivity among women has profound implications for the dynamics of intimate relationships, reshaping the roles and expectations of both partners. As women become more discerning in their choice of mates, men are compelled to rise to the challenge and demonstrate their value and desirability through their actions and behaviors.

High-value men are characterized by their confidence, ambition, physical attractiveness, and social status. They may find themselves in greater demand among women seeking partners who offer the greatest potential for long-term satisfaction and fulfillment. Men who fail to meet these criteria may find themselves at a disadvantage in the competitive landscape of modern romance, facing increased scrutiny and competition from their peers.

Navigating the New Paradigm:

In light of these changes, men must adapt their approach to dating and relationships to thrive in the modern sexual marketplace. This may involve cultivating qualities such as confidence, ambition, emotional intelligence, physical fitness, and masculinity (Buss, 2016).

You must be willing to invest in yourself and your personal growth, continually striving to become the best version of yourself in order to attract high-value partners who are physically attractive and youthful and share your hopes and dreams. By embracing the principles of self-improvement, you can position yourself for success in forming lasting relationships with high-value women or even for brief sexual encounters with them.

CHAPTER 8

Beauty in the Digital Era: Evolutionary Shifts in Women's Mate Choice on Online Dating Platforms

In the ever-evolving digital realm of online dating, the interplay between evolutionary dictates and technological advancements continues to shape the landscape of modern romance. This chapter delves into how these factors intersect, shedding light on women's mate choice, particularly emphasizing the increasing significance of physical attractiveness in the selection process.

Mate preferences are deeply ingrained in strategies honed over millennia. Historically, women's attraction to physically dominant and assertive men served as a survival mechanism, signaling genetic fitness and the ability to provide protection and resources in ancestral environments (Buss, 1989).

However, the digital era, particularly with the rise of online dating platforms, has thrown a curveball into traditional evolutionary processes. While evolutionary instincts have long influenced mate selection and still do, the online realm has amplified the importance of physical attractiveness as a determinant of desirability among women. This shift can be attributed to the visual nature of online dating, where profile pictures take center stage, overshadowing other evolutionary cues like social dominance and provisioning abilities (Hitsch et al., 2010).

We cannot overlook the inherent gender disparity on online dating platforms, where men outnumber women significantly. This lopsided ratio influences mate choice dynamics, particularly affecting the average man's experience in the digital dating scene. With fewer women compared to men, competition for female attention intensifies, posing challenges for men who do not fit conventional attractiveness or social status norms (Bruch & Newman, 2018).

Historically, men have been more inclined to engage in competitive behaviors, including pursuing mates through various avenues like online dating. Additionally, societal norms may encourage men to take the lead in seeking romantic connections, leading to higher male participation rates on these platforms (Finkel et al., 2012).

Online dating's proliferation has birthed the paradox of choice, leaving individuals overwhelmed by the abundance of options. For women, this paradox is magnified due to the gender disparity, inundating them with messages and inquiries from male suitors.

In this saturated environment, women's selectivity peaks as they sift through potential partners, filtering based on evolutionary cues of physical attractiveness. Men not meeting these criteria may find themselves sidelined in favor of those perceived as high-value mates, perpetuating the emphasis on looks in mate selection (Todd et al., 2007).

Social media and online platforms wield significant influence over how women perceive attractiveness and choose partners. It is important to recognize how exposure to online attention can warp women's views, leading to inflated self-perception and heightened expectations for high-value partners.

Whether on social media platforms or dating apps, online platforms have become a central arena for communication and self-expression. For women, these platforms offer a constant influx of validation and admiration, fostering a sense of entitlement and superiority. The rush of likes, comments, and messages fuels a dopamine-driven cycle, distorting perceptions of attractiveness and raising the bar for potential partners (Valkenburg & Peter, 2007).

While online validation may temporarily boost self-esteem, it also fosters a culture of comparison and superficiality. Women are inundated with images of idealized beauty, leading to feelings of inadequacy and insecurity. In response, women may adopt performative behaviors to enhance their online presence, perpetuating unrealistic standards and expectations (Fardouly et al., 2015).

For men navigating the digital dating landscape, it is essential to approach women's perceptions of attractiveness with discernment. While online attention may inflate egos and foster unrealistic expectations, it does not necessarily reflect genuine desires or intentions. By prioritizing authenticity, self-improvement, and meaningful connections, men can stand out amidst the noise of online validation and attract women who value substance over surface. You can show yourself to hold high value, while you develop high value, and secure female attention.

In today's digital dating scene, social media and online platforms wield significant influence over how women perceive attractiveness and choose partners.

Online platforms grant women access to a such a wide pool of potential partners, that they are extremely discerning in their choices. Faced with numerous options, women meticulously assess profiles, seeking partners who exhibit traits of compatibility and high value. While selectivity can be beneficial, it may also hinder women's quest for genuine connections.

In the dynamic realm of dating, women often navigate encounters where they are pursued by men who appear more physically attractive or financially affluent. This influx of temporary attention can create deceptive perceptions of their own value in the dating arena, fostering inflated self-esteem and misplaced confidence.

Women frequently encounter situations where they attract the interest of high value men who are more physically attractive or possess greater material resources. This superficial allure can be compelling, drawing women into interactions that promise excitement and validation based on external qualities rather than deeper connection or compatibility (Li et al., 2013).

Temporary attention from men perceived as more attractive can create unrealistic impressions of worth, leading women to overestimate their attractiveness and desirability in future dating interactions. This mismatch between perceived and actual desirability levels can contribute to disappointment and frustration when subsequent experiences fail to meet inflated self-perceptions (Todd et al., 2007).

One contributing factor to women's challenges in online dating is the differential impact of short-term encounters on mate value. While men may experience minimal repercussions from engaging in casual encounters, women risk potential devaluation of their mate worth. Higher-value men may temporarily lower their standards for short-term encounters, whereas women are often reluctant to compromise their mate value for fleeting connections, leading to a mismatch in expectations and desires (Birnbaum, 2017). In short, women will not typically have sex with men of lower mate value, but higher mate value men will have often have sex with lower mate value women, while excluding them from consideration as a partner.

Despite the allure of online dating, it is crucial to recognize that digital interactions are merely a prelude to real-world relationships. While women exercise selectivity online, true compatibility is tested offline, where individuals navigate face-to-face interactions and interpersonal dynamics. In this arena, men in their thirties and beyond often gain an advantage, especially as women's desirability peaks in their twenties (Belot & Fidrmuc, 2017).

Those men who are average in mate value get little to no responses and feel unsatisfied. But moderate to high value men can get who they want, and what they want, even if they have to put more effort in than a high value woman has to. They certainly have the advantage over average mate value women. High value men can be the clear winners in online dating if they know how to use dating sites to showcase their high value traits. So curate your online presence, get professional and flattering photos made or ones where you are doing activities, or are surrounded by friends. These types of photos are what give social proof of your high value and attractiveness. Write a profile that shows you as high value. When this is the man you show women you are, or are aspiring to be, you win.

CHAPTER 9

Unraveling Female Autonomy and Where Men Win

In modern relationships, understanding the evolving dynamics of female autonomy is crucial for men seeking to navigate the complexities of dating and partnership. It is essential to dissect how women's increasing independence has reshaped the landscape of attraction, intimacy, and commitment.

Historically, men have traditionally occupied the role of providers and protectors within relationships, while women relied on them for survival and security (Buss, 1989). However, the feminist movements of the twentieth and twenty-first centuries have brought about significant changes in gender dynamics, granting women greater access to education, employment, and economic independence (Becker & Moen, 1999), as we have discussed earlier. This newfound autonomy has undoubtedly empowered women, but it also necessitates a reconsideration of traditional gender roles and their implications for relationships.

With the increasing independence of women, there has been a notable shift in their attitudes and behaviors within relationships (England, Allison, & Wu, 2007). Women now also prioritize qualities such as emotional compatibility, shared values, and mutual respect in potential partners (Regan, Lakhanpal, & Anguiano, 2012). Furthermore, physical attractiveness and traditionally masculine traits have gained prominence in women's mate preferences (Buss & Barnes, 1986). While financial stability remains important, it is no longer the sole determinant of attractiveness in a mate for women (Eagly & Wood, 1999). This shift towards more diverse mate preferences reflects the evolving socio-economic landscape and the changing roles of men and women in modern society.

This means men need to meet more and more criteria to satisfy women, but women have not had to increase their attractiveness to men to nearly the same degree. Women say they want sensitive men, and kindness is proven to be attractive to women, but most women want masculine men no matter what "modern" women they say they want.

The rise of female autonomy is also evident in divorce trends, where women initiate approximately 75% of divorces. This phenomenon speaks to women's increasing agency and independence within relationships (Johnson & Rogers, 2017). Women are no longer willing to remain in unhappy or unfulfilling marriages, choosing instead to prioritize their own well-being and happiness (Goldberg & Carlson, 2014).

Research indicates that women are less inclined to remarry after divorce or widowhood compared to men, as they have reduced reliance on men for material support and less need for sex (Becker & Moen, 1999). This trend indicates women's commitment to their autonomy and personal fulfillment, as they prioritize themselves over traditional notions of partnership and companionship (Brown & Lin, 2012). Many men who seek companionship may find themselves left behind in this changing landscape, highlighting the importance of being a high-value partner (Baker & Emery, 2018).

Men have an advantage in attractiveness due to their longevity in maintaining appeal to potential partners, and existing partners. Let's delve into the factors that contribute to men's prolonged attractiveness and its implications for modern dating and partnership dynamics.

One of the key advantages men have in attractiveness is their ability to accrue resources and status as they age (Buss, 1989). Here we are talking about into their late 20s and through at least their late 30s.

Women may not need or want resources to the same degree anymore, but they still are attracted to them. Evolutionary psychology speculates that women have a predisposition to seek out mates who can provide resources and security, as these qualities were essential for ensuring the survival and well-being of themselves and their offspring throughout human history (Buss & Barnes, 1986). As men mature and establish themselves in their careers, they often gain access to greater financial resources and social status, making them more attractive to potential partners seeking stability and security in a relationship.

Men also maintain a level of physical attractiveness as they age that women do not, albeit through different mechanisms than women. While women's physical attractiveness may decline with age due to factors such as hormonal changes and loss of collagen, men often maintain their physical appearance well into their later years (Zebrowitz et al., 2013). Research has shown that men's attractiveness is often associated with traits such as maturity, confidence, and social status, which tend to improve with age (Fink et al., 2012). Also, men's ability to maintain physical fitness through regular exercise and healthy lifestyle choices can contribute to their enduring appeal to current and potential partners (Rikli & Jones, 2013).

While it is true that women place a higher value on looks than they used to, particularly in the context of short-term mating preferences and during periods of ovulation (Haselton & Gangestad, 2006), men still hold a significant advantage in attractiveness due to their prioritization of youth and fertility cues, which women do not value as much (Buss, 1989). As we have found, evolutionary psychology suggests that men are inherently drawn to physical traits associated with youth and fertility, such as clear skin, symmetrical features, and a healthy waist-to-hip ratio (Singh, 1993). These traits serve as fitness cues that signal a woman's reproductive potential and ability to bear healthy offspring, making them highly desirable to men seeking reproductive success.

For men navigating the complexities of modern dating and relationships, it is essential to recognize and leverage their advantage in attractiveness to cultivate genuine connections with potential partners, and ensure current relationships are strong. By focusing on self-improvement, personal growth, and the accumulation of resources and status, men can enhance their appeal and attract partners who value stability, security, and maturity in a relationship (Sprecher, 2014). Additionally, men can capitalize on their enduring physical attractiveness by maintaining their health, fitness, and confidence as they age, ensuring that they remain desirable to potential partners throughout their lives (Steverink, Lindenberg, & Ormel, 1998).

Key factors that contribute to men's enduring attractiveness are their maturity and confidence. As men age, they often gain a deeper understanding of themselves and the world around them, which translates into a sense of confidence and self-assurance that is highly attractive to partners (Orth et al., 2012). This maturity allows men to navigate the complexities of modern relationships with grace and poise, making them desirable companions for women seeking stability, security, and emotional fulfillment in a relationship.

The Importance of Social Status

Another factor that contributes to men's enduring appeal is their social status and success, which we will discuss more later. However, research has shown that women are often drawn to men who hold positions of power, influence, and authority, as these qualities are associated with stability, security, and resources (Townsend & Levy, 1990). As men age and establish themselves in their careers, they often gain access to greater financial resources and social status, making them more attractive to partners seeking long-term commitment and companionship.

For younger men, women are attracted to attributes indicating resource or provisioning potential, such as ambition and social status, which significantly influence their mate preferences and relationship choices (Buss, 1989; Li & Kenrick, 2006). This preference can impact younger men positively who demonstrate these qualities because they may be perceived as more desirable partners for long-term relationships or marriage, despite their age (Buss & Schmitt, 1993). Thus, younger men who exhibit traits associated with resource acquisition may appeal to women seeking stable and supportive partners.

The Maintenance of Physical Fitness

Regular exercise, healthy lifestyle choices, and self-care routines allow men to maintain their physical appearance as they age, ensuring they remain desirable to partners regardless of age (Booth et al., 2001).

The Disadvantage for Women

While men may maintain a level of physical attractiveness as they age, the emphasis on youth and beauty for evolutionary reasons places women at a disadvantage in attraction and mate selection. Women are often judged more harshly based on their physical appearance, as evolutionary preferences prioritize traits associated with youth and fertility in potential partners (Buss, 1989). This focus on youthful attributes may lead to greater scrutiny of women's appearance and less tolerance for signs of aging, compared to men who are perceived as maintaining attractiveness despite age-related changes.

Attractiveness in Middle Age

While women may have ways to extend their attractiveness into middle age, they pale in comparison to men's numerous strategies for enhancing their appeal and prolonging their attractiveness well into their later years.

We'll talk more about the strategies below more in depth later on and how to employ them.

As we have discussed, one of the key strategies is status, and this is even more true in middle age than at other points in a man's life. Men now more often hold positions of power, influence, and authority, that are qualities associated with stability, security, and resources (Buss, 1989). As men advance in their careers and establish themselves in their fields, they acquire greater financial resources and social status, enhancing their attractiveness to partners seeking long-term commitment, companionship, and ambition.

These men, buoyed by their career success and elevated social status, often attract younger women seeking partners who can provide security and stability (Hitsch et al., 2010). You do not need to partner with a middle aged woman, unless that is who you want, just because you are middle aged. A caveat: A study by Smith et al. (2020) indicated that women generally do not prefer men who are typically over 10 years older than themselves. Though this statistic doesn't always apply to all men, especially high value men.

Strength training, cardiovascular exercise, and flexibility routines can help men build and maintain muscle mass, improve posture, and enhance overall physical appearance, making them more desirable to partners seeking fitness and vitality in a relationship (Dionigi & Baker, 2020).

Fashion and grooming also play a significant role in enhancing male attractiveness in middle age. Investing in well-fitted clothing, and grooming routines can help men elevate their appearance and confidence, making them more attractive to partners (Kwak & Zinkiewicz, 2009).

Confidence and self-esteem are essential qualities that contribute to male attractiveness in middle age (Dworkin et al., 2015). Men who exude confidence and self-assurance are inherently more attractive to partners, as they convey a sense of strength, stability, and assertiveness. Building confidence can be achieved through various means, including setting and achieving goals, overcoming challenges and obstacles, and cultivating a positive mindset and self-image (Baldwin & Lin, 2008).

By investing in physical fitness and health, embracing fashion and grooming, building confidence and self-esteem, and leveraging evolutionary attractive qualities while focusing on self-improvement, personal growth, and cultivating genuine connections with partners, you can enhance your overall attractiveness and appeal well into your later years and secure meaningful relationships or short-term liaisons.

The Challenges of Maintaining Female Attractiveness in Middle Age

In modern dating and relationships, women encounter unique challenges as they age, rooted in evolutionary dictates that shape perceptions of attractiveness. While men may have many strategies for improving their appeal, women often contend with evolutionary pressures that influence societal norms and expectations surrounding age and beauty.

One of the ongoing challenges women encounter as they age is the impact of evolutionary pressures on societal perceptions of attractiveness. Throughout history, men have been instinctively drawn to traits associated with youth and fertility, which are seen as markers of reproductive success (Buss, 2016). Consequently, women often feel pressured to maintain a youthful appearance as they grow older, influenced by evolutionary instincts that prioritize traits linked to reproductive potential. Women exhibiting signs of youth and fertility, such as clear skin and symmetrical features, are perceived as more attractive to potential partners. However, as women age and experience decline in these physical markers, they may face increased competition from younger, more fertile counterparts.

Unlike men, who may have various strategies for enhancing their attractiveness in middle age, women often face limitations rooted in evolutionary adaptations. While men can accumulate resources, invest in physical fitness, and embrace fashion and grooming, women may find themselves constrained by evolutionary expectations that prioritize youth and fertility (Buss, 2003). The emphasis on these traits may limit women's options for enhancing their attractiveness and lead to feelings of inadequacy and insecurity as they age.

Women encounter distinct evolutionary challenges as they navigate attractiveness in middle age. These challenges are deeply rooted in the evolutionary pressures that have shaped human mating behavior over millennia.

Research suggests that women typically reach peak attractiveness in their late teens to early twenties, with attractiveness gradually declining over time due to hormonal changes and societal perceptions of beauty brought on due to the natural, evolutionarily developed preferences of men. In contrast, men tend to maintain attractiveness into middle age, with traits such as maturity and social status contributing to their enduring appeal (Buss, 2003). Men define what is attractive about women, and women define what is attractive about men.

As individuals age, the dynamics of power and influence in romantic relationships undergo a subtle shift. While women may hold advantages in physical attractiveness and fertility in their younger years, men often gain the upper hand as they accrue resources and status. This shift typically occurs in men's thirties to forties, making them more desirable partners in the dating market.

Middle aged divorced women with children have it hardest of all, research consistently shows that women face greater challenges in the dating scene after a divorce, because they typically have primary custody of children and the attendant responsibilities that go with that. Studies indicate that single mothers often encounter difficulties in forming new romantic relationships compared to single fathers. For instance, research by Sweeney (2010) highlights that women with children are viewed as less desirable partners due to perceived time constraints and responsibilities associated with parenting.

Revisiting Mate Preferences

In the past, women were attracted to men who could provide resources and security, as these qualities were essential for ensuring the survival of themselves and their offspring. However, with the rise of female autonomy, women no longer rely solely on men for financial stability. This shift has led to a reevaluation of women's mate preferences, with women seeking emotional compatibility, shared values, and mutual respect, yet they also want men with traditionally attractive masculine traits that are counter to their other preferences in a mate. Additionally, women now prioritize men's looks more than they used to, as the need for material support diminishes.

While women are still attracted to men with resources, their need for material support has diminished, leading to a new approach to relationships where emotional fulfillment and physical attraction can outweigh financial security. Women always value kindness in a mate, but not feminized men like so many claim to. This all results in men having to fulfill too many roles to satisfy a woman in a long-term relationship and a woman saying and thinking she wants one thing but really desiring another.

CHAPTER 10

How to Become a High Value Man: Strategies

Evolutionary Significance of Women's Preference for Confident Men

We talked earlier about how confidence is very attractive to women. Confidence has long been recognized as an attractive trait in potential partners, rooted deeply in our evolutionary past.

Assertiveness, self-assurance, and a sense of dominance are qualities that were advantageous in ancestral environments where resources were scarce and competition was intense (Snyder et al., 2008; Cheng et al., 2013). Women evolved to be attracted to men displaying confidence, as it signaled the ability to acquire resources, provide protection, and navigate social hierarchies effectively, thereby enhancing survival and reproductive success (Trivers, 1972; Hill et al., 2013).

Social dominance, leadership, and resilience indicate genetic fitness and overall health (Judge & Bono, 2001; Cheng et al., 2013). From an evolutionary perspective, women are naturally drawn to men who exhibit confidence, as it suggests robust genetic qualities that increase the likelihood of healthy off-spring and reproductive success (Fisher et al., 2005; Cheng et al., 2013).

Confident individuals are often perceived as leaders and influencers within social groups, which confers advantages in mate selection and reproductive success (Cheng et al., 2013; Henrich & Gil-White, 2001). Men displaying confidence are more likely to attract mates and establish social dominance, leading to increased access to resources, mating opportunities, and reproductive success. Women are evolutionarily predisposed to be attracted to confident men, as they offer assurances of status, protection, and provisioning for themselves and their offspring (Hill et al., 2013; Cheng et al., 2013).

Confidence plays a pivotal role in shaping interpersonal relationships and mate selection dynamics. Confident men are adept at asserting their needs, communicating effectively, and navigating social interactions, traits highly valued in potential partners (Buss & Shackelford, 2008; Cheng et al., 2013). Women naturally gravitate towards confident men, as they provide stability, security, and assertiveness in relationships, fostering successful pair bonding and reproductive success (Cheng et al., 2013).

Building Self-Esteem and Confidence

Having self-esteem is key to having confidence. One way you can increase your self-esteem is through self-reflection and introspection. Taking the time to examine your beliefs, values, strengths, and weaknesses can provide valuable insights into areas for personal growth and improvement. By identifying areas where you excel and areas where you may need to improve, you can develop a more balanced and realistic view of yourself, to identify areas of strength and where there is room for improvement.

Setting and achieving goals is another effective strategy for building self-esteem and confidence (Judge & Bono, 2001). Accomplishing goals provides a sense of purpose, direction, and accomplishment, demonstrating competence and resilience, which are attractive qualities to women. You can accomplish goals at work, through hobbies, or even by volunteering for charitable causes.

Positive self-talk is essential for maintaining healthy self-esteem and confidence (Wood et al., 2009). By replacing negative thoughts with affirming and empowering statements, you can cultivate a more positive inner dialogue, bolstering your confidence and resilience in social interactions. There are many ways to do this. You can do this through reading books on affirmation, going to church, apps like Calm or ThinkUp, or through telling yourself that you are strong and capable every day. You can write a list of all the affirmations you have received from work in emails, cards from loved ones, compliments you have received, or by recollection of what people have said your strengths are. There are many ways to cultivate positive thoughts, you have to find ways that work for you. I have found repeating in my head, several times a day, that I am strong and can handle anything has helped me exhibit stronger behavior when accompanied by standing up straight with my shoulders confidently held back.

One concept I have explored and applied is that of establishing myself as my primary point of mental reference. This principle entails remaining steadfast in my decisions and emotions without allowing external influences, particularly from others, to sway or dictate them. It involves observing others' behavior, yet internally reflecting on whether their actions warrant a response that aligns with my personal values and objectives.

This necessitates disregarding bad behaviors and the unnecessary stress they induce, and results in my asserting personal autonomy over life choices and outcomes. If your wife is angry at you unreasonably, for instance, you don't necessarily need to make her problem yours.

Consistently reinforcing this mindset involves constantly questioning your alignment with this principle: "Am I placing myself as my mental point of origin?" If found lacking, internal recalibration precedes any deliberate response, ensuring that actions are only taken when necessary for rectifying mistakes, which you should address. So don't be unkind or controlling.

But by adopting this approach, you can cultivate self-respect, and garner respect from others, especially women.

Stepping out of comfort zones is crucial for personal growth and development also (Seery et al., 2010). Embracing uncertainty and trying new experiences helps you expand your comfort zones, and can increase your confidence in navigating unfamiliar situations. Have you ever thought of rock climbing, or learning a new language? Whatever it is, get uncomfortable to grow.

Assertiveness and boundary-setting are key skills for navigating relationships (Baumeister et al., 2016). By expressing your thoughts, feelings, and needs clearly and respectfully, you can build mutual respect and understanding with women, fostering healthy and fulfilling relationships.

Raising your self-esteem and confidence are essential for success with women. By incorporating strategies such as self-reflection, goal-setting, positive self-talk, stepping out of comfort zones, and practicing assertiveness and boundary-setting, you can enhance your attractiveness and authenticity, leading to more meaningful connections with women. Empowered with self-assurance and self-worth, you can approach dating and relationships with confidence, integrity, and authenticity, ultimately fostering fulfilling connections with women.

If you need to fake confidence until you make it, that is okay. Practice these methods, and there are others:

Command Attention: Walk into a room with purpose. Hold your head high, make eye contact, and let your presence be known.

Master Your Style: Dress sharp and own your look. Confidence starts with feeling good about how you present yourself. We will talk more about this later.

Speak with Authority: Project your voice, speak clearly, and do not hesitate. Your words should command attention and respect.

Take up Space: Do not shrink back. Expand your posture, spread out comfortably, and show that you are comfortable in your environment.

Embrace Your Uniqueness and Masculinity: Celebrate what makes you different. Confidence stems from embracing your individuality and strengths. Also, be masculine, assertive, decisive, and bold.

Handle Setbacks Gracefully: Learn from failures and setbacks without letting them shake your self-assurance. Use setbacks as fuel for future success.

Know Your Worth: Understand your value and do not settle for less. Confidence comes from knowing you deserve the best.

Lead the Way: Take initiative and lead by example. Confidence shines through when you are willing to take charge and guide others.

Stay Cool under Pressure: Keep your composure in stressful situations. Confidence shows when you can handle challenges with grace and poise.

Something to note is that studies indicate that in the short term, and especially for purely sexual encounters, a woman may be initially attracted to displays of confidence and self-assuredness that are extreme or cocky. Women tend to like "bad boys" when they are ovulating. These traits can pique initial interest due to their association with social dominance and potential advantages in resource acquisition. (Farrelly et al. 2017, and Dufner et al., 2013).

The Evolutionary Drive behind Women's Attraction to Men with High Status

The allure of status in the realm of attraction has deep roots in our evolutionary past, shaping the preferences and behaviors of both men and women.

High-status men often possess greater access to resources, wealth, and social capital, attributes that were highly advantageous in ancestral environments where survival and reproductive success were closely linked to resource acquisition and provisioning (Buss, 1989). As we've said before, but it bears repeating as we dig deeper, women evolved to be attracted to men with high status, as they offered greater assurances of access to resources, protection, and support for themselves and their offspring. From an evolutionary perspective, selecting a mate with high status increased the likelihood of survival and reproductive success, thus perpetuating this preference over generations.

Status is often associated with traits such as intelligence, ambition, and leadership, which indicate genetic fitness and overall quality (Fisher et al., 2005). Women are naturally drawn to men with high status, as it signals genetic superiority and the ability to thrive in competitive environments.

High-status men often occupy positions of leadership, influence, and dominance within social hierarchies, which can confer advantages in mate selection and reproductive success (Mazur, 1985). Women are naturally attracted to men with high status, as they offer greater assurances of social dominance, protection, and provisioning within their communities. Selecting a mate with high status allowed women to align themselves with powerful and influential partners, increasing their access to resources, mating opportunities, and social support networks.

The selection of mates with high status has significant implications for offspring fitness and survival. High-status men are more likely to provide resources, protection, and support for their offspring, increasing their chances of survival and reproductive success (Daly & Wilson, 1988).

Women's attraction to men with high status is deeply rooted in our evolutionary history, shaped by adaptive pressures that favored traits associated with resource acquisition, genetic fitness, and social dominance.

Understanding How to Use Status

One of the primary ways men can accumulate status is through education and career advancement. Pursuing higher education, obtaining advanced degrees, and excelling in one's chosen field can elevate a man's professional status and earning potential, thereby increasing his attractiveness to women seeking partners with ambition, drive, and financial stability (Judge & Bono, 2001). For those unable to attain advanced degrees, attending workshops, seminars, or enrolling in online courses in relevant fields may give sufficient proof of ambition and a trajectory toward career development.

Wealth and financial stability are key components of status that can significantly impact a man's attractiveness and desirability to women. Accumulating wealth through strategic investments, entrepreneurship, getting a promotion, making a good salary, getting a new job earning more money, and financial planning can provide you with the means to live a comfortable and fulfilling lifestyle, which is appealing to women seeking partners who can provide security and stability (Nettle, 2005). Even if your financial resources are limited, until you can create resources, you can cultivate the look of success by the way you dress and the way you carry yourself can help create the illusion of wealth and stability.

Social connections and networks are another essential aspect of status that can build your attractiveness and success with women. Building and cultivating relationships with influential individuals, industry leaders, and community members can provide you with access to valuable resources, opportunities, and social capital (Heaphy & Dutton, 2008). Attending networking events, joining professional organizations, and engaging with influential figures on social media platforms can create the perception of a well-connected and influential social network while you build one from those efforts.

Leadership and influence are qualities that are highly attractive to women seeking partners with confidence, assertiveness, and charisma. Men who demonstrate leadership abilities, take initiative, and inspire others are perceived as more attractive and desirable mates (Bass, 1990). Even if you do not hold formal leadership positions, taking charge of social situations, organizing group activities, or leading discussions on topics of interest can give you a chance to show leadership and influence.

In some situations, faking status may be necessary to increase one's attractiveness and success with women, while one works to legitimately attain status, because you cannot fake status forever if you are looking for a relationship. This can involve embellishing your achievements, inflating your social standing, or presenting a carefully curated image of success and influence. While honesty and authenticity are paramount in forming genuine connections, strategically positioning yourself as confident, ambitious, and successful, without outright lying, can create initial attraction and intrigue, paving the way for deeper connections to develop over time, while also creating the chance for access to short term sexual encounters.

Accumulating status is a powerful way for men to enhance their attractiveness and success with women. By investing in education and career advancement, building wealth and financial stability, cultivating social connections and networks, and demonstrating leadership and influence, men can elevate their perceived value and desirability as potential partners.

Evolutionary Origins of Women's Preference for Athletic Men or Fit Men

Let's dive deeper into the evolutionary origins of how women's preference for athletic men provides valuable insight into underlying motivations and drivers.

Throughout human history, survival and reproductive fitness have been paramount concerns (Apicella et al., 2007; Courtiol et al., 2010). Athleticism and physical prowess were essential for hunting, gathering, and defending against predators and rivals. Women evolved to be attracted to men who displayed traits associated with athleticism, such as strength, agility, and endurance, as these qualities signaled an increased likelihood of survival and reproductive success for both themselves and their offspring.

Athleticism is often correlated with overall health and vitality (Booth et al., 1999; Shoup & Gallup, 2008). From an evolutionary standpoint, women are naturally drawn to men who exhibit signs of good health, as this suggests genetic fitness and the ability to provide for and protect potential offspring. The physical fitness and prowess demonstrated by athletic men signal vigor, resilience, and genetic quality, making them desirable mates from an evolutionary perspective.

In ancestral environments where resources were scarce and competition was fierce, athletic prowess conferred advantages in resource acquisition and provisioning (Apicella et al., 2007;

Puts et al., 2010). Men who were physically fit and capable were better equipped to hunt for food, gather resources, and provide protection for their families and communities. Women evolved to be attracted to men who displayed traits associated with athleticism, as they offered a higher likelihood of survival and reproductive success for themselves and their offspring.

Women's preference for athletic men can be understood as a product of evolutionary pressures that favored traits associated with physical fitness and prowess. From an evolutionary perspective, this increased the likelihood of reproductive success and the survival of offspring, thus perpetuating these preferences over generations.

From signaling health and strength to enhancing survival and provisioning capabilities, athleticism has long been associated with desirable mate qualities that increase the likelihood of reproductive success.

Physical Fitness and Women's Preferences

While men may perceive extreme muscularity as the epitome of attractiveness, women's preferences are nuanced and diverse. Here is what you need to know about women's preferences and attraction:

Appreciation for Thin Men with Balanced Physique: Contrary to popular belief, most women are drawn to men with a balanced and proportionate physique rather than extreme muscularity. A toned and athletic physique is often more appealing to women than excessive muscle mass, as it conveys health and athleticism (Frederick et al., 2007). Focus on developing a V-shaped torso through resistance training, which includes broad shoulders and a narrower waist, as this is often perceived as attractive by women (Frederick et al., 2007).

Personality and Confidence Matter: Ultimately, a man's personality, confidence, and demeanor play a significant role in his attractiveness to women (Back et al., 2011). Focus on cultivating confidence, authenticity, and a positive attitude, as these qualities are universally appealing and can grow your attractiveness to women regardless of your physique (Back et al., 2011).

Achieving physical fitness and attractiveness is within reach for men through realistic strategies that prioritize health, balance, and well-being. By incorporating resistance training, embracing a balanced diet, and understanding women's preferences, men can optimize their physical appearance and increase their appeal to potential partners.

If you are overweight and unable to lose weight, you should consider a GLP-1 medication. They are revolutionarily effective. These medications can, and most of the time do, cause 15%—25% total body weight loss, according to the Cleveland Clinic and GoodRx. The two most effective are semaglutide (patented name is either Ozempic or Wegovy) and tirzepatide (patented name is either Monjuaro or Zepbound).

These drugs are very expensive, and not all insurance covers these medications, but you can look for coupons. As of the writing of this book, you can try compounded versions of the active ingredients for about half the price through licensed healthcare professionals and FDA-regulated compounding pharmacies. These medications are only allowed to be compounded when there is a shortage, as there is now, because these drugs are patented. You need only search online to find the compounded versions.

Do not attempt to get these medications without a prescription from a legitimate pharmacy as with websites that offer "medication" without a prescription are dangerous. You never know what you are getting.

There are some risks with compounded medications because the FDA cannot approve compounded medications for safety and efficacy because they are not mass produced and are made in smaller batches. However, when you use a reputable provider online, that connects you with a licensed health care professional, and an FDA-regulated pharmacy – you should be fine.

Anecdotally, compounded medications worked for me because they have the active ingredients in the patented drugs. I lost 15% of my body weight in several months and look and feel great. I am at my ideal weight.

As for body shape, the way to improve that is to get in the gym. If you have persistent body shape issues CoolSculpting or Emsculpting can be very useful, but they are expensive. You can look those treatments up.

Still, the most recognized method for body shaping involves engaging in gym workouts, or performing resistance training at home using weights.

Creativity Is Attractive

Creativity is a potent aphrodisiac that ignites passion, intrigue, and connection. For the average man, tapping into his creative potential can be a transformative journey that captivates the hearts and minds of women. Whether it is writing poetry, playing music, painting, or pursuing any other form of artistic expression, creativity offers a powerful means of self-expression and connection.

Research indicates that creativity can enhance perceived attractiveness and appeal to potential partners (Leder et al., 2006; Kaufman & Kaufman, 2018). Creative individuals are often viewed as more interesting, open-minded, and capable of expressing emotions effectively, which can foster attraction.

Explore your interests and passions to uncover your creative spark. Experiment with different artistic mediums to find those that resonate with you, and allow you to express yourself authentically. Embrace vulnerability and authenticity in your creative pursuits, allowing yourself to explore new ideas, perspectives, and emotions.

The Irresistible Allure of Romance: Unveiling Its Charms to Women

Few elements hold as much sway as romance.

At the heart of romance lies the promise of emotional connection and intimacy, which are fundamental human needs. Women are naturally drawn to men who demonstrate an ability to connect on a deep emotional level, as it fosters a sense of closeness, understanding, and vulnerability (Hazan & Shaver, 1987; Acevedo et al., 2012). Romance offers a pathway to cultivate meaningful connections and build intimacy through gestures of affection, kindness, and thoughtfulness.

Romance is a language of love and devotion, expressed through words, actions, and gestures that convey affection and admiration. Women are deeply moved by expressions of love and devotion, as it signifies commitment, loyalty, and most importantly investment in the relationship (Gonzaga et al., 2008; Gable et al., 2004). From handwritten love letters to spontaneous acts of romance, men who demonstrate their love and devotion in meaningful ways capture the hearts of women and leave a lasting impression.

Romance has the power to create memorable moments that linger in the hearts and minds of women long after they occur. Whether you create a romantic candlelit dinner, a surprise weekend getaway, or an authentic declaration of love, these moments leave an indelible mark and strengthen the bond between partners (Aron et al., 2000; Lewandowski Jr & Bizzoco, 2007). Women are enchanted by the magic of romance, as it creates opportunities for shared experiences, laughter, and joy that enrich the relationship and create cherished memories.

In the small moments of everyday life, woven into the fabric of daily interactions and gestures of affection romance thrives. Women appreciate men who make an effort to keep the flame of romance alive, whether it is through simple acts of kindness like writing a note and telling her how you feel about her by leaving notes on her car seat before she leaves for work, heartfelt compliments, or something else, this is where creativity comes in (Reis & Clark, 2013; Impett et al., 2005). Also, just by cultivating an atmosphere of romance in everyday life, you can deepen your connection with women and create a relationship filled with love, passion, and mutual appreciation.

However, it is important to note that while romance is a powerful tool for deepening connections, it typically enhances existing attraction rather than creating it from scratch. Research suggests that initial attraction often involves physical and psychological factors beyond romance alone (Eastwick et al., 2011; Finkel et al., 2007). Building rapport, shared values, mutual interests, and, not least of all, attraction are required to establish the groundwork for romantic gestures to have their desired impact.

In a world where romance is often seen as a lost art, men who embrace its charms hold the key to unlocking the hearts of women and cultivating relationships filled with love, passion, and romance.

However, you must be careful to not become overcome with romance to the point that you believe that there is only one perfect or ideal partner for yourself that cannot be replaced in any circumstances. This is a form of destiny belief or romantic fatalism. This perspective posits that each individual has a predestined or predetermined soulmate, and that finding this specific person is crucial for achieving long-term happiness and fulfillment in romantic relationships. Believing in a soulmate is not scientific, but there is nothing wrong with believing in one.

Believing in poetry is not scientific either. Some parts of life are better left to poetry. But this book is not about poetry.

Romantic fatalism often involves a strong belief in the concept of "the one," where individuals perceive their soulmate as uniquely compatible and irreplaceable, possessing qualities that perfectly complement their own (Knee et al., 2008). This belief can lead to a heightened sense of emotional investment and dedication to a particular partner, as well as a reluctance to consider alternative romantic possibilities.

Psychologically, romantic fatalism may stem from a combination of factors, including cultural influences, personal experiences, and attachment styles (Slotter & Gardner, 2012). For some individuals, the belief in a singular soulmate may provide a sense of security and meaning in their romantic pursuits, reinforcing a narrative of romantic destiny or cosmic alignment.

From a scientific perspective, research suggests that the belief in romantic destiny can influence relationship outcomes and perceptions of partner compatibility (Finkel et al., 2015). While this belief can foster deep emotional connection and commitment, it may also contribute to unrealistic expectations and vulnerability to disappointment if the relationship does not meet idealized standards.

Addressing romantic fatalism involves promoting a balanced perspective on relationships, emphasizing the importance of compatibility, mutual respect, and shared values in fostering healthy and fulfilling romantic connections (Knee et al., 2008). You must maintain open communication, cultivate personal growth, and explore diverse relationship opportunities because this can help mitigate the potential negative effects of rigid beliefs about romantic destiny on emotional well-being and relationship satisfaction.

Never give a woman the power of thinking that you cannot find another woman, or be okay without her. Men who exude confidence in their ability to attract new partners may indirectly signal qualities such as genetic fitness, resource acquisition, and social dominance, which are attractive to women seeking high-quality mates (Buss, 1989). These traits historically have contributed to reproductive success and offspring survival, making them desirable in partners and potential partners. This does not mean you should make your partner feel insecure but you should know you can always find someone new, and the woman you are with should believe that if you had to, you could.

The Allure of Style: Embracing Fashion, Grooming, and Facial Hair

Style serves as a powerful tool for enhancing one's allure and charisma

Fashion and grooming offer a canvas for self-expression and individuality, allowing you to showcase your unique personality, style, and confidence (Tiggemann & Boundy, 2008; Swami et al., 2009). Women are naturally drawn to men who take pride in their appearance and exude confidence in their sense of style. Embracing fashion and grooming allows you to present yourself in the best possible light, signaling attention to detail, self-assurance, and sophistication.

Fashion and grooming have the power to optimize a man's physical attractiveness and highlight his best features (Gueguen, 2012; Rantala et al., 2013). Well-fitted clothing and grooming techniques such as skincare, hairstyling, and grooming facial hair can accentuate your facial structure, physique, and overall appearance. Women are naturally drawn to men who take care of themselves and present themselves in a polished and put-to-gether manner.

Fashion and grooming serve as markers of social status and cultural capital, signaling sophistication, refinement, and social savvy (Swami et al., 2009; Townsend & Levy, 1990). Men who embrace fashion trends, cultivate a signature style and groom themselves with care project an image of success, taste, and discernment that is inherently attractive to women. You can read up on what is fashionable, stay true to your own style, but be intentional in the way you present yourself. By aligning your appearance with societal norms and expectations, you can intensify your perceived status and desirability as a partner.

Facial hair, in particular, holds a special allure that can significantly increase a man's attractiveness. Facial hair adds depth, masculinity, and character to a man's appearance (Dixson et al., 2016; Dixson & Brooks, 2013). Women are particularly drawn to stubble or a trim and light beard, as it signals maturity, masculinity, and virility. Experimenting with different styles of well groomed facial hair, grooming techniques, and maintenance routines can allow you to find the perfect balance that complements your facial features and personal style.

The Power of Scent: Harnessing Fragrance for Seduction

Studies have shown that women may be subconsciously drawn to men whose scent indicates genetic compatibility and immune system diversity, which are factors linked to offspring health (Havlíček & Roberts, 2009; Rikowski & Grammer, 1999). Additionally, scent can enhance perceptions of masculinity and attractiveness, highlighting its role as a subtle yet powerful factor in human mate choice (Santos et al., 2016). You can take a shower, but you cannot change your scent to make it genetically compatible. However, you can do things to please women with your scent.

It's relevant because scent plays a profound role in attraction, women generally possess a keener sense of smell compared to men, as evidenced by studies showing women outperforming men in various olfactory tasks, such as odor detection and discrimination (Doty et al., 1984; Brand & Millot, 2001).

Scents also evoke emotions, memories, and desires in those who encounter it. By harnessing the power of fragrance, men can create a lasting impression and evoke positive associations in the minds of women (Havlicek et al., 2005; Hare, 2011).

Invest in high-quality colognes with appealing scents that complement your personality and style. Choose subtle, sophisticated fragrances that leave a lingering trail of allure and intrigue wherever you go.

The Evolutionary Appeal of Mental Strength

From the earliest days of our ancestors, women have been instinctively drawn to men who possess mental strength, emotional intelligence, and inner fortitude.

Throughout human history, the ability to withstand adversity and overcome challenges has been a crucial determinant of survival and reproductive success. Men who exhibit mental strength—resilience, determination, and emotional stability—are better equipped to navigate the challenges of life, providing protection, security, and support to their partners and offspring. Women, attuned to the cues of mental strength, are naturally drawn to men who exude confidence, stability, and resilience in the face of adversity.

Research by Kalisch et al. (2015) highlights that resilience, defined as the ability to adapt to stress and adversity, is associated with better psychological well-being and relationship satisfaction, which are attractive traits in potential partners.

Emotional intelligence, the ability to understand and manage one's own emotions as well as empathize with the emotions of others, is a highly prized quality in romantic partners. Men who possess emotional intelligence are adept at navigating the complexities of interpersonal relationships, fostering trust, intimacy, and connection with their partners. Women, seeking companions who can provide emotional support and understanding, are naturally drawn to men who exhibit empathy, compassion, and emotional intelligence.

A study by Brackett and Mayer (2003) suggests that emotional intelligence contributes significantly to relationship quality by enhancing communication, empathy, and conflict resolution skills, which are crucial for maintaining long-term romantic bonds.

To show strength emotionally, listen attentively, validate feelings, and express empathy and compassion in your interactions. Also, learn the same behaviors the earlier section on confidence addresses.

Understanding Why Women Laugh at Men They're Attracted To

Humor is attractive to women, and funny men win hearts. We have touched on humor, but let's explore further: women's laughter in response to men they are attracted to serves as a non-verbal cue signaling interest and rapport (Hall et al., 2010). When a woman laughs at your jokes or finds you amusing, it is a sign that she enjoys your company and feels comfortable in your presence. By understanding the underlying reasons why women laugh at men they are attracted to, you can capitalize on this attraction and use humor to deepen your connection and build romantic chemistry.

Laughter is a social behavior that fosters positive interactions and signifies enjoyment of the other person's company. A woman's laughter at your jokes or humorous remarks indicates that she finds you engaging and likable, which can pave the way for deeper connection and romantic interest.

Humor plays a crucial role in enhancing a man's attractiveness to women (Wilbur & Campbell, 2011). Men who exhibit a sense of humor are perceived as more charismatic, confident, and socially adept, qualities that are highly desirable in potential romantic partners.

Laughter facilitates emotional connection and intimacy between romantic partners (Bressler et al., 2006). When a woman laughs in response to a man she is attracted to, it creates a shared experience of joy and amusement, fostering a positive emotional connection. This emotional bond can deepen over time as humor continues to play a role in their interactions, strengthening the romantic chemistry between them.

Laughter in social interactions often indicates a sense of ease and mutual understanding, suggesting that both parties are comfortable being themselves around each other.

Understanding why women laugh at men they are attracted to provides valuable insights into the dynamics of romantic attraction. By leveraging humor effectively, men can not only elicit laughter but also strengthen their connection with women, ultimately paving the way for deeper and more meaningful relationships.

To Be Funnier to Women

Spontaneity in humor delivery can be appealing. Women often appreciate wit that arises naturally in conversation, as it signals quick thinking and intelligence (Bressler, Martin, & Balshine, 2006).

Self-deprecating humor can be endearing, as it demonstrates humility and confidence simultaneously (Küfner et al., 2014).

Emotional intelligence is crucial; being attuned to social cues and knowing when humor is appropriate can make humor more enjoyable and less risky (Gifford & Dean, 2017). Context and timing are key; understanding situational dynamics and adjusting humor accordingly can increase its effectiveness and perceived charm (Gervais & Wilson, 2005). If you work on emotional intelligence and confidence, you will understand how to accomplish this better.

Incorporating these strategies into interactions can help you engage women more effectively through humor, foster positive social connections, and potentially enhance attraction.

Mastering the Art of Conversation: Engage and Captivate

Effective communication is essential for building attraction and rapport with women. Master the art of conversation by honing your listening skills, asking thoughtful questions, and engaging in meaningful dialogue (Reese et al., 2013; Weger et al., 2014). Share stories, experiences, and passions that showcase your personality, interests, and values. Be attentive, witty, and charismatic in your interactions, leaving a lasting impression that sparks curiosity and interest in women.

The Art of Flirtation: Sparking Chemistry and Excitement

Flirtation is a playful and dynamic way to create chemistry and excitement in interactions with women (Hall & Xing,

2015; Hall et al., 2010). Use humor, teasing, and playful banter to create tension and intrigue, igniting sparks of attraction and interest. Be confident, charming, and lighthearted in your approach, allowing your flirtatious energy to create a sense of anticipation and excitement. Embrace the thrill of the chase, leaving women eager for more of your captivating charm and charisma.

You may find it valuable to pretend that you are a younger child or teenager version of yourself teasing a younger version of the woman you are trying to build rapport with. But be careful because there is a fine line between teasing and making fun of a woman, whereby she may take offense.

Building the Attraction: Short-term Encounters, Initial Attraction, and Approaching Women

Research consistently underscores the importance of assertiveness and confidence in men's approaches toward women. According to Simpson et al. (1990), men who display their confidence when initiating romantic interactions are generally perceived more positively, as this trait enhances perceptions of attractiveness and sincerity. Approaching a woman directly to ask for a date in an appropriate venue with confidence gives you better chances of garnering interest in a date, or in an interaction that can lead to a sexual encounter. Just ask a woman out if you are interested, it is a numbers game and you likely will be told no more than yes. Do not be dissuaded from trying.

Clear communication of romantic intentions is crucial. Eastwick and Finkel (2008) highlight that directly expressing interest reduces ambiguity and fosters a more positive response from potential partners. Additionally, studies by Grammer et al. (2000) suggest that women often find assertive and socially dominant behaviors appealing during initial encounters, which can be communicated through confident and direct communication styles. So be direct in your approach, when you ask for a date make your intentions clear. But don't be overly eager because that is not attractive in initial encounters.

Non-verbal cues such as body language, eye contact, and facial expressions also play a significant role in conveying confidence and sincerity, as noted by Hall et al. (2015). Do not be afraid to look a woman in the eye and linger there just a little more than you normally would in an interaction with someone you are not interested in. Your body should face hers. Broaden your shoulders, stand up straight, and make yourself look confident physically, but not intimidating.

Presenting yourself positively through grooming, attire, and overall demeanor can significantly enhance initial attractiveness and leave a favorable impression, as supported by research from Back et al. (2011). You should look your best and be in a good mood, even if you have to pretend.

Exhibiting confident behavior, even if you do not feel confident or have not built confidence, is of the utmost importance. You need to be assertive. You must be clear in your communication, and be positive in your self-presentation to be successful in your interactions and to build initial attraction.

These behaviors have a better chance of success when you are high value or at least have worked on developing some high value traits.

Overall, while confidence and directness can increase the likelihood of success when men ask women out, it's essential to balance assertiveness with respect for boundaries and receptiveness to social cues. For instance, you do not want to get fired for sexual harassment because you were too forward in the workplace. Effective communication and a genuine interest in understanding the other person's feelings and preferences are crucial for building positive interactions that can lead to a date or a sexual interaction.

Mate Maintenance Strategy: Communication, Silence, and Withdrawal in Relationships

Effective communication allows individuals to convey their needs, preferences, and emotions, thereby fostering mutual understanding and enhancing relationship stability (Buss, 2019).

Research underscores the importance of communication in relationship satisfaction and longevity. For instance, studies have shown that couples who engage in open and constructive communication tend to report higher levels of relationship satisfaction (Gottman & Silver, 1999). From an evolutionary standpoint, effective communication may signal compatibility and cooperation between partners, traits that are advantageous for raising offspring and ensuring familial harmony (Bower et al., 2019). Communication is important for you and your partner to participate in.

Moreover, communication serves as a tool for negotiating conflicts and resolving issues within relationships. Evolutionarily, men who can effectively communicate and negotiate are better equipped to navigate challenges and maintain social alliances, which may have conferred survival and reproductive advantages in ancestral environments (Campbell et al., 2002).

The dynamics of communication within relationships are crucial for mate selection and maintaining reproductive success. Effective communication allows individuals to convey their needs, preferences, and emotions, thereby fostering mutual understanding and enhancing relationship stability (Buss, 2019).

However, sometimes communication is not the answer. From an evolutionary psychology perspective, communication within relationships can be understood through the lens of mate selection and maintenance strategies. Men and women often employ different tactics rooted in evolutionary history to maximize reproductive success and relationship stability.

One intriguing strategy observed in some men is selectively choosing to be silent or ignore their partner, particularly when their needs are not being met despite repeated attempts to communicate. Research suggests that intermittent withdrawal or selective silence can serve several functions in a relationship. It can create a psychological space where the woman may begin to reevaluate her behavior and responses to her partner's needs. Evolutionarily, this mirrors the concept of "mate choice copying," where individuals observe and adjust their behaviors based on the actions of others in the social environment, potentially increasing the likelihood of alignment with their partner's preferences over time (Bower et al., 2019; Maner et al., 2010).

Periodic silence or withdrawal may also foster a sense of longing or desire in the woman, enhancing her motivation to meet her partner's needs in order to regain his attention and favor. This can be understood in terms of reinforcement theory, where intermittent reinforcement (in this case, intermittent attention and silence) can strengthen the desired behavior (meeting the partner's needs) more effectively than constant reinforcement (always being available and responsive) (Skinner, 1953; Bower et al., 2019).

Women, more so than men, may be particularly attuned to relational dynamics and responsive to cues of emotional availability and stability in their partners. This sensitivity may be rooted in ancestral contexts where women relied on consistent support and investment from their male partners for survival and reproductive success (Buss, 2019). Men who demonstrate emotional control and calmness in the face of relationship challenges may signal greater emotional stability and maturity, which are desirable traits in a long-term partner.

This demeanor can enhance a woman's perception of her partner's ability to handle stress and adversity, potentially increasing her feelings of security and trust in the relationship (Campbell et al., 2002; Gottman & Silver, 1999).

While every relationship is unique and communication styles vary, there are evolutionary insights that shed light on why some men may choose to be selectively silent or withdraw at times when their needs are not being met. Talking too much can make things worse sometimes.

These strategies, when used judiciously and with empathy, can influence a woman's behavior positively over time, potentially increasing her responsiveness to her partner's needs and enhancing overall relationship satisfaction. However, it is essential to use these tactics as a last resort and to be strategic and not manipulative, when using this approach. It is not manipulative if used this way, it means you have exhausted communication and it is not working. You are simply not participating until your needs get met when communication has not worked. You have to approach this behavior without expectations and as a way to concentrate on yourself and what makes you happy if your needs aren't being met despite communication having been tried. In extreme cases you may need to employ pulling away for a prolonged period of time allowing you time to work on yourself and to concentrate on what you enjoy, while improving yourself, in case you find yourself single again. In this case, you need to become stronger and independent. If your partner meets your needs then you can be pleasantly surprised and begin communicating more regularly again.

You must always remember though that healthy communication and mutual understanding remain fundamental for maintaining a balanced and fulfilling relationship and that employing silence and withdrawal in the wrong situation will backfire on you. So be sure that your partner is not in a place where this behavior would alienate her further unless you this is an acceptable risk for you. If you want out of the relationship entirely, you should end your relationship through transparent communication.

The Evolutionary Appeal of Kindness in Human Courtship

In the ancestral environment, where survival depended on cooperation and mutual support, kindness emerged as a crucial trait for fostering social cohesion and group harmony (Fletcher et al., 2015). Women as primary caregivers and nurturers were naturally inclined to seek out mates who displayed kindness and compassion, as these traits signaled a willingness to provide care and protection for offspring (Eisenberg et al., 2006). By selecting kind and altruistic mates, women could ensure the survival and well-being of their offspring, thereby enhancing their reproductive success.

Kindness serves as a reliable indicator of good genes and parental investment potential in prospective mates (Farrelly et al., 2019). Men who demonstrate kindness and compassion are perceived as more likely to be reliable partners and caregivers, capable of providing support and protection for their offspring.

Women, attuned to these cues of parental investment, are naturally drawn to kind and nurturing men, as they offer a higher likelihood of successful reproduction and offspring survival. Thus, kindness becomes a desirable trait in the context of mate selection, signaling genetic fitness and parental investment potential.

It's important to note that these factors are especially pertinent in long-term relationships rather than short-term encounters. In short-term situations, excessive kindness can sometimes be perceived negatively and hurt your chances of success in sexual encounters.

Being kind plays a pivotal role in fostering social bonds and created cooperative relationships within ancestral communities (Hruschka et al., 2014). Men who exhibit kindness and altruism are more likely to form positive social connections and alliances, which can confer a range of benefits, including access to resources, protection from threats, and increased reproductive opportunities. Women, seeking partners who can contribute to their social and material well-being, are naturally drawn to men who display kindness and generosity, as these traits indicate a capacity for forming and maintaining supportive social networks.

In the ancestral environment, where resources were scarce and threats were ever-present, cooperation and mutual support were essential for survival (Barclay, 2016). Men who demonstrated kindness and altruism were more likely to not harm their mates, collaborate with others, mitigate conflict, and navigate social challenges effectively. Women, seeking partners who could contribute to their safety and security, were naturally drawn to men who displayed these cooperative and prosocial behaviors, as they offered a higher likelihood of successful cooperation and conflict resolution.

Kindness serves as a catalyst for fostering emotional intimacy and trust in romantic relationships (Ditzen et al., 2008). Men who demonstrate kindness and compassion create a nurturing and supportive environment that promotes emotional connection and bonding with their partners. Women, seeking emotional fulfillment and security in their relationships, are naturally drawn to men who exhibit these caring and empathetic qualities, as they offer a deeper sense of emotional intimacy and connection.

The evolutionary roots of women's attraction to kindness can be traced back to our ancestral past, where kindness served as a reliable indicator of genetic fitness, parental investment potential, and social cooperation. By selecting kind and nurturing mates, women could increase their reproductive success and offspring survival, thereby shaping the evolution of human mating preferences. Today, the allure of kindness continues to exert a powerful influence over women's mate choice, serving as a cornerstone of successful and fulfilling romantic relationships.

To embody kindness in the context of human courtship, you can actively demonstrate empathy through emotional intelligence toward the woman you are with, showing generosity towards others, and your partner. This could involve actively listening to your partner's needs and concerns, offering emotional support during difficult times, and showing appreciation through thoughtful gestures and acts of kindness.

So, there you have it. You have a better understanding of women now, why they act the way they do, and what their preferences and drives are from a scientific standpoint. You know when mating what they are looking for. Hopefully, you have some idea of what you need to do to attract the nice and high value women that you are, every man is, attracted to. Women not high in mate value must compromise and seek out men lacking some of the adaptive male traits we have gone over. Most middle aged women must compromise far more. With this knowledge, you do not have to compromise what you value most in a mate.

Women are knowable, and anybody who tells you differently is misinformed, or buying into the idea that everything is a societal construct. This book shows you that attraction is all based on science, and all of it is discernable. Everything in mating is related to evolutionary adaptations, not societal changes. Societal changes can alter behavior to a degree, but it cannot erase what evolution has made us attracted to through tens and tens of thousands of years of evolutionary adaptation.

Online dating and other changes in society prove that certain evolution driven attributes can be artificially changed. But it remains that modern women say they want a man who can cry, but they really want a strong man. Women may say they do not care about what job you have, but they care very much. Or at least the women you want to date, marry, have sex with do.

Women do not know what they actually want, but now you do. Society can shuffle the deck, but it cannot make new cards.

Even the seismic changes in society that came about with the women's liberation movement in the 1960s were related in large part to a pill that affected hormones. Remember hormones play a pivotal role in transmitting a woman's evolved sexual preferences, influencing attraction and mate selection based on indicators of genetic fitness and reproductive potential.

You do not need to develop all of the attributes and behaviors listed in this book to increase your attractiveness to women, some improvement may be enough and what, if anything, you decide to change will depend on your personal goals.

This book is a beginning. It helps you understand what women are attracted to and how they approach sexuality from a scientific place. It incorporates some practical suggestions, but you need to figure out how to put them into place.

If you are not a high value man yet, know that you can become one.

I hope this book helps you in your sexual and romantic relationships with women. At the very least, I hope you found it interesting and enlightening.

<u>Thank you so much for reading this book. If you enjoyed this book, please consider reviewing it, or at least rating it.</u> By doing so you'll be helping men like yourself, and like I was before I had this researched knowledge. Men will find value in understanding women in ways that are currently hidden from them. You will help them open their eyes. You can be a part of the success of this book, and the transformative information inside of it for other men, so if it helped you please think about reviewing it. This information changed my life, it was instrumental in improving my marriage. I had to research for years to understand all of it, to connect the dots I've connected. I wanted to give this information to other men, that's the reason I've written this book. You can make a difference too. Share this information with other men, and I'd appreciate you leaving a review (or at least a rating) to encourage other men to read it, if you are open to that. Thank you.

– Cole Hunter